Hotdish Mania

Edited by
Pat Dennis

HOTDISH HAIKU Copyright @2005 by Pat Dennis (All individual haiku copyrights are owned by individual authors.)

Printed in the United States of America. All rights reserved. No part of this book may be used or reproduced in any manner whatsoever without written permission except in the case of brief quotations embodied in critical articles or reviews. For information address Penury Press LLC, P O Box 23058, Richfield, MN 55423

Pat Dennis, Editor
Bobbye Johnson, Director of Development
(www.bobbyejohnson.com)

Penury Press LLC
P.O. Box 23058
Richfield MN 55423

www.penurypress.com
pat@penurypress.com

First Edition
10 9 8 7 6 5 4 3 2 1

Library of Congress 2005906397

ISBN: 978-0-9676344-3-2
ISBN: 0-9676344-3-1

Cynthia Rykken, Original Cover Design
Spring Book Design, Cover Consultant/
Production
(www.springbookdesign.com)

To Howard Johnson, Ret.

燦

Why Hotdish Haiku?

The poets of Hotdish Haiku use the smallest literary form of poetry–haiku–to explain the biggest mystery of cuisine known to mankind–hotdish.

Similar to a casserole, in fact exactly like a casserole, hotdish is the term used in the Upper Midwest to describe a baked dish that is usually based on a cream-of-something soup and combined with a few other ingredients like rice, beef and canned vegetables.

The dish originated with thrifty housewives who knew that a little bit of this, and a little bit of that, meant a lot of something served in a dish, hot. For over half a century, hotdish has been served at weddings, funerals, baby showers, potlucks, office parties, and family dinners. It is a welcomed member of any family, like an old Uncle who is likeable but cheap, very cheap.

From one generation to the next, hotdish recipes were shared, meals were enjoyed, and waistlines expanded. Hotdish became more then an entree. It shifted into nostalgia and became a favorite memory of childhood and gatherings of love. And needless to write, culinary judgment quickly disappeared. Hotdish became synonymous to family, friends, and community. It jumped from the bottom of the food chain and entered into the consciousness of spiritual circles; especially those located in church basements.

Haiku's spiritual roots are connected to the Japanese Zen monks who created the contemplative poetry that emphasizes the philosophy of being in the moment. Because of the brevity of haiku, the poetry is not complicated with metaphors and literary distractions. It is, instead, an "ah-ha" experience of the sudden understanding of the nature of things. It is an instant reminder that all is right with the world. It is, as if, when someone writes or utters–"I do remember, at my favorite Aunt's wedding, a hotdish was served"–the universe produces a collective sigh.

The poets of Hotdish Haiku invite you to be in the moment with hotdish.

HAIKU

Casserole displayed
Gratification delayed
Tongue needs oven mitt

Dean Johnson

Where else can olives,
Okra, Gouda, and eggplant
Achieve nirvana?

Jeremy Yoder

Herds of Lutherans
Running to church hotdishes
Natural stampede

Pat Dennis

Dogs howling at dusk
Cats chase invisible mice
Hamburger crumbles

Mary Hirsch

Ironic, I find
Someone at my church potluck
Steals my spatula

Codey Livingood

Theatre attendees
Avant-garde enthusiasts
Yet, they eat hotdish

Pat Dennis

New recipe fails
Yet all not lost for in street
Pothole needs filling

Jeremy Yoder

Mittens on the stove
Tears trickle down the windows
Memory's hot dish

Marilyn Victor

Mercury dropping
A bushel of fallen leaves
Deluge of noodles

Dean Johnson

A mid-morning prayer
Christian ladies on their knees
Still, hotdish is served

Pat Dennis

Not just funerals
Good for both weddings and wakes
Hotdish and sheet cake

Lance Zarimba

Leftover hotdish
Eaten every night this week
Bathroom scale proves it

Codey Livingood

First day meal delight
Second day is better yet
Third day could cause death

Wendy Nelson

Snow with rabbit prints
And then a few of my own
It's bunny hotdish

Pat Dennis

Company coming
Add rice, soy, peas, and bean sprouts
Serve Oriental

Peggy Jaegly

Last minute potluck
Clean out frig of leftovers
Bake with soup and chips

Lance Zarimba

Precious (tater) tots
This is a reason to live
In Minnesota?

Pat Dennis

Eat all the hotdish
Since the remains for a week
Will be leftovers

Jeremy Yoder

Noodles with tuna
Potato chips are crumbled
A hotdish is topped

Sandra Thomas

Traffic snarls 'round me
Time drifts past my window shield
Save me tater tots

Mary Hirsch

Summer memories
Childhood of tuna noodles
Knew not–just say no

Pat Dennis

Chefs sniff at "hotdish"
"Casserole" is too cheesy
Celebrate the cheese

Mary Monica Pulver

Cat has disappeared
Macaroni noodles boil
No tuna – surprise!

Mary Hirsch

Five on Thursday night
Panic, run to neighbor's house
Borrow canned tuna

Marit Livingood

Cover comes off dish
Steam rises expectation
Salad abdicates

Dean Johnson

Quality of life
Fishing, hiking, museums
But Five Can Hotdish?

Pat Dennis

Ten kinds of hotdish
Bingo and cigarette smoke
Catholic party

Pat Dennis

He left in the spring
I would have cried except for
Soothing words...cream of

Pat Dennis

Sunday dreams call me
Toes grasp the tender green grass
Cream of mushroom soup

Mary Hirsch

Cans of soup and beans
Dented and sold on clearance
Served to Minister

Pat Dennis

Craving hotdish now
Out of cream of mushroom soup.
Might as well be dead.

Dale Wolf

Can being opened
She always serves a hotdish
Divorce will follow

Pat Dennis

Meat, potatoes, salt
Mom's secret ingredient
Cream of mushroom soup

Thea Miller Ryan

Taters, beef, mushrooms,
Drop from my fork to the floor
Here, Kitty, Kitty!

Codey Livingood

Deer on a highway
Swerving left, then right, a crash
Roadkill hotdish–yum

Pat Dennis

Pennant race is done
There is no joy in Mudville
Hotdish brings it home

Mary Hirsch

Glistening noodles
Brown ground beef nudges green beans
Condensed soup, seeping

Marit Livingood

Out-of-state transplant
Alone, sad, yet remember
Antidote–hotdish

Pat Dennis

Kitchen dilemma
Mix vegetables, cheese and rice
Dinner is ready

Peggy Jaegly

Some call it crummy
My favorite hotdish top
I say gratineed

Dean Johnson

Vietnamese, Thai
French, Italian, fab cuisines
Then why, why hotdish?

Pat Dennis

Viva Las Vegas
Elvis has left the building
Love me tater tot

Mary Hirsch

The times are changin'
Where have all the noodles gone
Hotdish daddy-o

Mary Hirsch

Big fish swimming caught
Chopped, onion, pepper, egg, soup
Casserole complete

Peggy Jaegly

Over and over again
Cold milk, hotdish, bars, coffee
The circle of life

Pat Dennis

My pantry weeps for
Creamy soup, freezer holds no
Tater tots, eat out

Dale Wolf

Ghost of old hotdish
Memories from a childhood
Glass dish with cover

Sandra Thomas

Cream of mushroom urge
Onions, ground meat, white rice baked
Now, where are the Tums?

Pat Dennis

Beware church potluck
Many pots to be tasted
Yet no luck in sight

Jeremy Yoder

Funeral again
Tin foiled pans wait in the church
Hotdish to die for

Thea Miller Ryan

Recipes

Crouching Chicken–Hidden Veggies

2 cups cooked chicken
3/4-cup mayonnaise
1 cup mushrooms, sliced
1 can cream of chicken soup
1 cup chopped celery
1 can chow mein noodles

Preheat oven to 350 degrees.

Dice chicken. Mix all ingredients together. Bake at 350 degrees for 30 minutes.

Seven Samurai's 5-Can Hotdish

1 small can turkey or chicken
1 can cream of chicken soup
1 can cream of mushroom soup
1 can chow mein noodles
1 small can evaporated milk

Preheat oven to 350 degrees.

Mix all together. Pour into buttered casserole dish. Bake at 350 degrees for 25 minutes.

Reincarnated Hotdish

1/4 cup honey
3 celery stalks, chopped
10 oz can chicken
1 can cream of mushroom soup
1 can cream of chicken soup
1/4 cup milk
1 medium onion, chopped
1/4 cup soy sauce
1 tsp ginger
4 cups chow mein noodles
1/2 cup cashews

Preheat oven to 350 degrees.

Mix everything except noodles and cashews together in a 2-quart baking dish. Salt & pepper to taste. Bake 30 minutes at 350 degrees. Stir in noodles and cashews and bake another 15 minutes.

Nirvana in Pyrex

3 cups cooked chicken, diced
1 tbsp soy sauce
2 tsp fresh lemon juice
1-1/4 cups diced celery
1/3 cup sliced green onions
1 can bean sprouts, drained
1 can water chestnuts, sliced
Salt/pepper
3/4 cup mayonnaise
1/3 cup chopped toasted almonds
1 can chow mein noodles

Preheat oven to 350 degrees.

Sprinkle chicken with soy sauce and lemon juice. Cover and chill for at least 2 hours. Add remaining , except almonds and noodles. Spoon into buttered 1-1/2 quart casserole and sprinkle with almonds. Bake at 350 degrees for 30 to 35 minutes. Serve on crisp chow mein noodles.

Geisha-To-Go

1-1/2 lbs ground turkey
1 small onion, chopped
1/2 cup chopped celery
1 can sliced water chestnuts
1 can sliced mushrooms
2/3 cups raw rice
1 tsp salt
1 tsp pepper
1/3 cup soy sauce

Preheat oven to 350 degrees.

Open cans of water chestnuts and mushrooms. Drain and reserve liquid. Brown turkey, onion, and celery in a skillet; drain off fat. Add water chestnuts, mushrooms, rice, salt, pepper, and soy sauce to turkey mixture. Add enough water to reserved liquids to make 2 cups. Stir into turkey mixture. Cover and bake at 350 degrees for about an hour.

Fortune Cookie Hotdish

1 can cream of celery soup
1/3 cup water
1/3 cup salted cashews
2 tbsp soy sauce
2 green onions, sliced
1 can Chinese vegetables
2 cups cooked chicken
2 cups hot cooked rice
Fortune cookies

Preheat oven to 350 degrees.

Dice chicken. Mix soup, water, soy sauce, cashews, green onions, vegetables, chicken and rice in 2-quart baking dish. Bake at 350 degrees for 25 minutes or until hot. Stir. Remove from oven. Serve with fortune cookies.

Sumo Fisherman Hotdish

1 lb fresh sliced broccoli
1-1/2 cups cooked chicken
1 can cream of broccoli soup
1/3 cup milk
1/2 cup shredded Cheddar cheese
2 tbsp dry breadcrumbs
1 tbsp butter, melted

Preheat oven to 450 degrees.

Sauté broccoli until tender. Cube chicken. Arrange broccoli and chicken in a 2-quart baking dish. In a small bowl combine soup and milk. Pour over broccoli and chicken. Sprinkle Cheddar cheese on top. Combine breadcrumbs with melted butter and spread over cheese. Bake at 450 degrees for 20 minutes or until bubbling.

House of Blue Tums Hotdish

1 small bag Tater Tots
1 bag Chinese vegetables
1 bag California blend frozen
  vegetables
1 can green beans
1 can cream of mushroom soup
2 lbs ground beef
8 oz Cheddar cheese

Preheat oven to 350 degrees.

Drain green beans and reserve liquid. Brown ground beef. Thaw vegetables in microwave. Put vegetables and green beans in greased 2-quart baking dish. Mix green bean juice, soup and pour over vegetables. Add ground beef, cheddar cheese, and then Tater Tots. Bake at 350 degrees for 1 hour.

Mama San(derson) Hotdish

1 lb ground beef
1 onion, chopped
2 stalks celery, chopped
½ cup slivered almonds
1 cup cooked rice
1 can cream of chicken soup
½ cup water
3 tbsp soy sauce
1 can chow mein noodles

Preheat oven to 350 degrees.

In a large skillet sauté the ground beef. Add onion and celery sauté until tender. In a separate bowl, combine almonds, rice, soup, water and soy sauce. Mix together well and add to the beef mixture. Transfer to a greased 2-quart casserole dish. Top with chow mein noodles. Bake at 350 for 30 minutes.

King Kong's Favorite Hotdish

Potatoes (raw) sliced thin
1 pkg. frozen Japanese vegetables, thawed
1 lb ground beef
1 medium onion, chopped
Pinch of salt
Pepper
1 can tomato soup
Water
Dill weed
1 large can mushrooms or fresh mushrooms

Preheat oven to 350 degrees.

Arrange thick layer of raw sliced potatoes in buttered casserole dish. Place thawed vegetables mixed with mushrooms on top of potatoes. Brown ground beef and onions and then spread on top of vegetables. Salt and pepper. Mix can of soup with equal amount of water. Pour soup mixture over entire dish and sprinkle dill weed on top. Bake, covered, for 60 minutes and 15 more minutes uncovered.

Holy Mantra Hotdish

1-1/2 lbs ground beef
1 large onion, chopped
1 can cream of mushroom soup
1 can chicken with rice soup
1 can water
1-cup raw, uncooked rice
2 cups chopped celery
5 tbsp soy sauce
1 can bean sprouts, drained and rinsed
1 large can chow mein noodles

Preheat oven to 325 degrees.

Brown ground beef with onion, salt and pepper. Add cans of soups, water, rice, celery, soy sauce and bean sprouts. Salt and pepper to taste. Bake at 325 degrees for 2 hours. Top with chow mein noodles and return to oven for a few minutes.

Shogun's Bingo Night Hotdish

1 1/2 lbs ground beef
1 large onion, diced
2 cups diced celery
1 can of tomato soup
1 can cream of mushroom soup
1 can of bean sprouts (drained)

Preheat oven to 350 degrees.

Sauté ground beef until brown. Mix together with diced onion, celery, tomato soup, cream of mushroom soup, and drained can of bean sprouts. Place in a greased 2-quart casserole. Cover top with chow mein noodles. Bake at 350 degrees for 40 minutes.

East Meets Midwest

1 can cream of chicken soup
1 cup shredded Cheddar cheese
1 pkg California blend vegetables
1 cup cooked rice
1 cup cooked ham, cubed

Preheat oven to 350 degrees

In a large saucepan, combine the soup and ½ cup of cheese. Cook and stir until cheese is melted. Microwave veggies until thawed. Stir in veggies, rice and ham. Put in a greased 1½ quart baking dish. Sprinkle with remaining cheese. Bake uncovered at 350 degrees for 25-30 minutes.

Okinawa Okay! Hotdish

1 can cream of mushroom soup
1/4 cup milk
1 tsp soy sauce
1 1/2 cup diced cooked pork roast
1/2 cup sliced celery
6 oz sliced water chestnuts
1/4 cup sliced green onions
2 tbsp chopped pimento
1 can chow mein noodles

Preheat oven to 375 degrees

Combine soup, milk and soy sauce. Add pork, celery, water chestnuts, green onion and pimento. Fold in 1 cup of chow mein noodles. Spoon into a shallow 1 ½-quart casserole or pie dish. Sprinkle with remaining noodles. Bake at 375 until thoroughly heated, about 20 minutes. Serve immediately.

Enlightened Pork

1 lb bulk pork sausage
1 bell pepper, chopped
1 can sliced mushrooms
2 tbsp soy sauce
1 medium chopped onion
6 oz of uncooked rice
8 oz of sliced water chestnuts
3 cups chicken broth

Crumble sausage into 2-quart casserole. Add onion, bell pepper, and drained mushrooms. Cover. Microwave on high for 5-7 minutes stirring once. Drain on paper towel, set aside. Combine soy sauce, rice, drained water chestnuts, and chicken broth. Cover and microwave on high for 6-7 minutes. Stir. Cover and microwave on medium, 50 percent power, for 30-35 minutes. Stir in sausage mix, cover and microwave on medium 10 minutes or until rice is tender and dry.

The Sound of One Spam Opening

1 can Spam
1 small can diced pineapple
1 medium chopped onion
1 clove garlic
1/4 cup vinegar
1/4 cup soy sauce
1 Tbsp Brown sugar
2 cups Chinese vegetables
2 cups cooked rice

Cook rice as according to direction on package. Sauté Chinese vegetables with onion and garlic. Add diced SPAM to vegetable mixture and sauté. Add vinegar, soy sauce and brown sugar. Add pineapple with juice and simmer to your taste. Serve over rice.

Be One With The Pork

1 can cream of mushroom soup
1 tsp curry powder
1-1/2 cups cooked pork, cut into
 small cubes
Salt & pepper
3 cups cooked rice
1 can peas, drained
1 cup diced carrots

Preheat oven to 350 degrees

Steam carrots until tender. In a small bowl, mix mushroom soup and curry powder. Combine the rest of the ingredients in a 2-quart baking dish. Salt and pepper to taste. Spread the soup and curry mixture over ingredients. Bake at 350 degrees for 30 to 40 minutes.

Bamboo Pork

2 lbs pork steak, cubed
2 large onions, chopped
1 cup celery, chopped
1 large green pepper, chopped
1 small can of mushrooms
1/2 red pepper chopped
2 cans chicken rice soup
2 cans cream of mushroom soup
1 cup water
1 cup uncooked rice

Preheat oven to 350 degrees

Brown pork steak cubes. Add chopped onions, cook until tender. Add the celery, green pepper, red pepper, mushrooms. Mix in 2 cans of chicken with rice soup and 2 cans of cream of mushroom soup, 1 cup water and 1 cup uncooked rice. Bake uncovered for 1½ hours at 350 degrees. Serve hotdish in bowls placed on bamboo placemats.

Koi Hotdish

1 16 oz pkg mixed vegetables
2 cans tuna in water, drained
1 cup uncooked instant rice
1 can cream of mushroom soup
1 cup milk
1 cup Goldfish Cheddar baked crackers

Mix vegetables, tuna, rice, soup, and milk in bowl. Spoon into 1 1/2 quart microwave-safe baking dish. Cover and microwave on high for 6 minutes. Stir. Cover and microwave 6 minutes more or until rice is tender. Stir and sprinkle top with goldfish crackers.

Kyoto Fishing Opener

4 oz medium egg noodles
1 can cream of shrimp soup
3/4 cup milk
1/2 cup mayonnaise
1 tbsp chopped green onion
1/4 cup diced celery
1/4 tsp salt
1/3 cup shredded Cheddar cheese
1 cup cooked shrimp
1/4 cup chow mein noodles

Preheat oven to 350 degrees

Cook noodles according to package directions; drain. Combine soup with milk, mayonnaise, onion, celery, and salt; mix well. Stir in cheese, shrimp, and cooked noodles. Turn into 1-1/2 quart casserole. Bake uncovered at 350 degrees for 30 to 35 minutes. Top with chow mein noodles; bake 10 minutes longer.

Lost In (Norwegian) Translation

1 cup chopped celery
1 cup cashews
2 tbsp minced dry onions
2 cup chow mein noodles
1/4 cup condensed milk
1 can cream of mushroom soup
14 oz canned tuna

Preheat oven to 375 degrees

Drain tuna and break apart. Mix milk and soup in a bowl. Add other ingredients, reserving 1 cup chow mein noodles, and mix well. Place in greased casserole dish and top with the reserved noodles. Bake 15-20 minutes at 375 degrees.

Emperor of South Dakota Hotdish

1 can tuna, drained
1 can pineapple chunks
1/3 cup blanched almonds, slivered
Salt & pepper to taste
1 package frozen peas, thawed
1 can cream of celery soup
1/4 cup pineapple chunks

Preheat oven to 325 degrees.

Combine tuna, pineapple, almonds, salt and pepper, peas and soup. Pour into 1-quart casserole. Top with pineapple. Bake at 325 for 20 minutes.

Yang no Yin Hotdish

4 cups diced celery
1/2 lb sliced fresh mushrooms,
1 small can sliced water chestnuts
2-3 large pieces of pimento
1 can cream of mushroom soup
1 cup Pepperidge Farm™ herb dressing
4 butter pats
1/2 cup blanched almonds
Salt & Pepper

Preheat oven to 400 degrees.

Drain water chestnuts. Dice pimentos. Sauté celery. In a large mixing bowl, combine drained celery with mushrooms, water chestnuts, pimento, soup, salt and pepper. Mix well and spoon into a sprayed shallow baking dish. Sprinkle the dressing over all, then top with the pats of butter. Top with almond accents. Bake at 400 degrees for 20-25 minutes.

Yin no Yang Hotdish

4-1/2 cups water
1 cup rice
2 cups reconstituted TVP
2/3 cup slivered blanched almonds
2 tbsp veggie "chicken" seasoning
1-1/2 cup chopped celery
1 large onion, chopped
1/2 cup chopped green pepper

Preheat oven to 350 degrees.

Bring water and seasoning to boil in a large saucepan. Add rice, cover and reduce heat, simmer 25 minutes or until water is absorbed. Remove from heat. Combine TVP (textured vegetable protein), onion, green pepper, and chicken veggie seasoning. Sauté in oil until tender. Add rice and 1/2 cup almonds to the vegetables. Mix well. Pour into 2-quart casserole. Sprinkle with remaining almonds. Bake at 350 degrees for 30 minutes.

Buddha's Lutefisk Delight

1 lb cooked broccoli spears
1 lb fresh cod
1 can cream of broccoli soup
1/3 cup milk
¼ cup shredded Cheddar cheese
2 tbsp dry breadcrumbs
1 tsp butter, melted
1/8 tsp paprika

Preheat oven to 450 degrees.

The delight in this dish is that there is no lutefisk. Lay broccoli in 2-quart shallow baking dish. Top with fish. Mix soup and milk and pour over fish. Sprinkle with cheese. Mix breadcrumbs, butter and paprika and sprinkle on top. Bake at 450 degrees for 20 minutes or until fish is done.

Yen for Hotdish

2 Chinese eggplants, diced
1/3 cup frozen peas
1 chopped scallion
1/2 cup water or vegetable broth
2 tbsp soy sauce
2 tbsp rice wine
1/2 tsp black bean Chili paste
1 tbsp cornstarch
Cooked Brown rice or cooked Japanese soba noodles

Put everything except the cornstarch mixture into the pot. Bring to a boil and simmer covered for 10 minutes. Mix cornstarch with water to form paste. Thicken the sauce with the cornstarch paste and serve with brown rice or Japanese soba noodles.

Buddhist Temple Basement Hotdish

2 Chinese eggplants
1 medium onion
1 medium green pepper
½ cup butter
1 egg, beaten
1 pkg. tube Ritz crackers

Preheat oven to 350 degrees.

Peel eggplants, slice and dice into ½-inch cubes. Chop the onions and green peppers. Put eggplant in medium saucepan with just enough water to cover. Bring to a boil and cook for 2-4 minutes. Drain in colander and allow to cool. Sauté onion and pepper in butter. Crush crackers. Put eggplant in mixing bowl and add pepper/onion mixture, crackers, and egg. Stir quickly until mixed. Put into a greased casserole dish and bake at 350 degrees for 30 minutes.

Northwood Ninja

1 tbsp. vegetable oil
1/2 cup chopped celery
1/4 cup chopped onion
1 can Cream of Broccoli soup
1/4 c. milk
6 oz Velveeta
1 (10 oz) pkg chopped broccoli
2 cup cooked rice

Preheat oven to 350 degrees.

Dice Velvetta. Thaw and drain broccoli. Sauté celery and onion until tender. Combine soup and milk; stir in celery-onion mixture, cheese, broccoli and rice. Pour into 10"x6" baking dish. Sprinkle with paprika. Bake at 350 degrees for 30 minutes or until hot.

Minnesota Mandarin

1 block firm tofu
1 cup mayonnaise
6 eggs
2 red peppers
2 cups snow pea pods
3 green onions
1 can water chestnuts
1 can Mandarin oranges
Hot mustard, oyster, or soy sauce

Preheat oven to 350 degrees.

Wrap tofu in cheesecloth and drain by setting 3 lbs weight on top of it. Let the tofu sit for 1 hour in a dish to catch liquid. Mash tofu in large bowl. Stir in mayonnaise. Stir in eggs until just mixed. Dice vegetables and then stir in vegetables into mixture. Grease 9 x 13 inch baking dish. Pour mixture into dish, and bake 1 hour at 350 degrees. Garnish with Mandarin orange slices. Serve with soy sauce and hot mustard or oyster sauce.

Mocking Seaweed

1 box Stove Top stuffing
1 pkg. drained frozen spinach
1 can cream of mushroom soup
4 oz Cheddar cheese, shredded
1 egg, beaten
1 tbsp onion, grated
Salt and pepper to taste

Preheat oven to 350 degrees

Mix Stove Top stuffing as directed. Mix all together. Salt and pepper to taste. Bake at 350 degrees for 30 minutes uncovered for crispness. (Cover at 15 minutes mark to make more moist.)

The Sort of Zen Masters

Jeremy Yoder used his dojo training to construct stories for the anthologies *Who Died in Here?*, *Cloaked in Shadow: Dark Tales of Elves*, and *Fantastical Visions III*. Yet enlightenment during Godzilla movies continues to evade him as he questions how hot it must get inside a rubber suit. (**www.jeremyyoder.net**)

Dean Johnson, when not writing Japanese poetry, is often available as a charming dinner guest. He lives in Minneapolis, Minnesota. (**www.deanjohnsoncomedy.com**)

Wendy Nelson knows that from place to place and lifetime to lifetime, she is a student of everything the universe has to teach. She enjoys spending both time and space with the merry band of souls she meets along the way.

Thea Miller Ryan enjoys the tranquil serenity of working at The Outdoor Campus in Sioux Falls, South Dakota. She spends many hours gazing out her prairie-view window, all the while pondering that earth-shaking question: Where can I find someone to build a 50-foot, anatomically correct largemouth bass? (**www.freewebs.com/theamillerryan**)

Marilyn Victor is a lapsed Lutheran who shivers at the sight of anything creamed. Her search for nirvana leads her to wild animal habitats throughout the world unless, of course, the animals are Protestant.

Mary Monica Pulver enjoys dishing the dirt, especially if it's hot. She lives in a cheesy suburb of Minneapolis where she writes needlework mysteries under a pseudonym which you may think of as a Parmesan shade tree, if you'd like. (www.Monica-Ferris.com)

Marit Livingood says she would make a poor Buddhist because, like an expensive vacuum cleaner, she has too many attachments. She has also achieved awareness that "Life is too short for uncomfortable shoes."

Lance Zarimba is a balanced Libra providing holistic therapy on a rehab unit. His meditations involve a "Therapy" mystery series. He has no Yin or Yang, but he does have a Riley and a Ripley. Their eight furry feet keep him busy and well grounded in the doghouse.

Mary Hirsch lives in Minneapolis, Minnesota and is a swell gal who, when not writing Haiku about food, spends her time writing humor, performing, getting in touch with her inner child, and trying to find her watch (which she loaned to that inner child). Visit www.maryhirsch.net to find out more about Mary — more than you'll really want to know.

Dale Wolf loved to write, draw, sing, watch Jeopardy, surf the web, play computer games, and eat frozen custard (not necessarily in that order). She passed away on December 31, 2004. You can read about her "playful romp" with breast cancer at http://www.caringbridge.org/mn/dalewolf/

Peggy Jaegly believes in infusing harmony in all aspects of her life, including eating good food and chocolate. She soothes patients at the bedside with her harp compositions and channels life's more challenging moments into short stories. Her latest mysteries can be found in *Who Died In Here?* by Penury Press, "Don't Break My Heart" in the *New Jersey Romance Writers Short Story Anniversary Anthology,* and "The Secret of Drumthwackett" in *Crime Scenes: New Jersey.*

Codey Livingood is a voicework artist, former stand-up comic, and holds a black-belt in Parcheesi. He often dreams of traveling to the Far East, but his alarm clock usually wakes him up before the plane lands. When not dropping things on the floor he divides his time between work, family, and surfing the net for the latest sightings of Bigfoot.

Sandra Thomas lives with her husband Glenn, daughter Mabel, and their two cats Elizabeth and Jessica in the Twin Cities. She has been eating hotdish since the early 60's and feels life is like hotdish– bland, warm and lumpy.

Pat Dennis is a practicing Buddhist Baptist, realizing in her dotage that accepting all beliefs and denying none is the most comfortable robe for her to wear. She continues to look for enlightenment everywhere, including HBO where the character Al Swearingin quipped, in an episode of *Deadwood,* "If you want to make God smile, tell him your plans."

HOTDISH TO DIE FOR

A hilarious, award-winning collection of culinary mystery short stories and 18 hotdish (casserole) recipes by Pat Dennis. Story titles include *Death by Idaho*, *Cabin Fever*, *The Elder Hostile*, *Hotdish To Die For*, *The Lutheran Who Lusted* and *The Maltese Tater Tot*.

"Always funny and often poignant, **Hotdish to Die For** serves up a healthy helping of stories that are truly Minnesota in their details and wonderfully universal in their appeal. This is a book to savor. I not only enjoy it, I've given it as a gift." William Kent Krueger, author of *The Devil's Bed*, *Purgatory Ridge*, *Boundary Waters,* and *Iron Lake*.

112 Pages, Paperback, ISBN 0-9676344-0-7. Retail Price $9.95. Available at local bookstores, online bookstores, and at penurypress.com. To order by mail send check or money order for $9.95 per book wanted plus $2.00 shipping and handling to: Penury Press, P O Box 23058, Richfield, MN 55423. (If Minnesota resident please add Minnesota state sales tax of 6.5% per book ordered.)

WHO DIED IN HERE?

An outstanding collection of 25 mystery short stories by 25 master storytellers of crimes and bathrooms, ranging from the zany to the deadly serious.

"...thoroughly fun anthology of 25 short stories of mystery, murder and crime by a wide variety of skilled storytellers...and every whodunit is connected somehow to bathrooms. An eyebrow-raising, tongue in check collection for mystery lovers."—*Midwest Book Review*

208 Pages Trade Paperback, Retail $12.95, ISBN 0-9676344-2-3

Available at local bookstores, online bookstores, and online at penurypress.com. To order by mail, send check or money order for $12.95 per book wanted plus $2.00 shipping and handling to: Penury Press, P O Box 23058, Richfield, MN 55423. (If Minnesota resident, please add Minnesota state sales tax of 6.5% per book.)

STAND-UP AND DIE

Stand-Up and Die is Pat Dennis' cozy mystery novel set in the funny yet dark world of stand-up comedy. Meet Mannie Grand, comedienne, self-confessed neurotic and amateur sleuth. When a fellow comic dies on stage Mannie is determined to find the killer. Follow her on a trail of murder, mayhem and mirth. Awarded the Merit Award for Fiction from the Midwest Publishers' Association. "Her characters are as wacky as one would expect from a professional comedienne. This book won't scare you from sleep, but it may make you die from laughing. We rated it four hearts."–*Heartland Reviews*.

208 Pages, Paperback, ISBN 0-9676344-10-5. Retail price $11.95.

Available at local bookstores, online bookstores, and online at penurypress.com. To order by mail, send check or money order for $11.95 per book wanted plus $2.00 shipping and handling to: Penury Press, P O Box 23058, Richfield, MN 55423. (If Minnesota resident, please add Minnesota state sales tax of 6.5% per book.)